Bonsai for Beginners

Mastering the Art of Growing and Caring for Bonsai Trees through an Exciting and Comprehensive Guide

Lucinda Hickman

Copyright 2023 – Lucinda Hickman © All rights reserved.

The content contained within this book may not be reproduced, duplicated, or transmitted without direct written permission from the author or the publisher. Under no circumstances will any blame or legal responsibility be held against the publisher, or author, for any damages, reparation, or monetary loss due to the information contained within this book. Either directly or indirectly.

Legal Notice:

This book is copyright protected. This book is only for personal use. You cannot amend, distribute, sell, use, quote or paraphrase any part, or the content within this book, without the consent of the author or publisher.

Table of Contents

LUCINDA HICKMAN 7

CHAPTER 1: INTRODUCTION. THE WORLD OF BONSAI 10

CHAPTER 2: THE CHOICE OF BONSAI 14

    MATERIALS FOR GROWING BONSAI 18

CHAPTER 3: THE BASICS OF BONSAI 21

    THE IDEAL LAND FOR BONSAI: TYPES, PROPERTIES, AND PREPARATION 22
    BONSAI WATERING: WHEN AND HOW TO WATER 24
    FERTILIZATION OF BONSAI: FREQUENCY, TYPES, AND DOSES 26
    BONSAI PRUNING CUTTING AND MODELING TECHNIQUES 27

CHAPTER 4: TRANSPLANTATION 29

    WHEN IS THE RIGHT TIME TO TRANSPLANT A BONSAI? 30
    HOW TO PREPARE BONSAI FOR TRANSPLANTING 31
    POST-TRANSPLANT CARE: WATERING, FERTILIZING, AND REST 35

CHAPTER 5: BUILDING THE TRUNK: TECHNIQUES OF WIRE, WEAVING, AND BANDAGING. 38

    HOW TO CHOOSE THE POSITION AND ANGLE OF THE TRUNK 39
    WIRE TECHNIQUES: HOW TO SHAPE THE TRUNK WITH COPPER WIRE. 41
    WEAVING TECHNIQUES: HOW TO SHAPE THE TRUNK BY INTERTWINING THE BRANCHES. ..43
    BANDAGING TECHNIQUES: HOW TO SHAPE THE TRUNK BY BENDING IT. 44

CHAPTER 6: CANOPY FORMATION: LEAF CUTTING, GREEN PRUNING, AND DEFOLIATION. 47

    LEAF-CUTTING TECHNIQUES: HOW TO SHAPE THE FOLIAGE BY CUTTING THE LEAVES. 49
    GREEN PRUNING TECHNIQUES 52

DEFOLIATION: WHEN AND HOW TO DEFOLIATE THE BONSAI 53

CHAPTER 7: DISEASE AND PEST MANAGEMENT: PREVENTION AND NATURAL REMEDIES 55

THE MAIN BONSAI PESTS AND HOW TO PREVENT THEM..57
NATURAL REMEDIES FOR BONSAI DISEASES AND PESTS..58
NEEM OIL 58
GARLIC 59
WATER AND SOAP 60
NETTLE 61
ACETIC ACID MORE DETAILS 62
CHAMOMILE..63
ALMOND OIL 64
GREEN TEA 65
COPPER 66
GINGER 67
ALOE VERA JUICE 67
HOW TO INTERVENE IN CASE OF PROBLEMS..68

CHAPTER 8: CLIMATE MANAGEMENT: EXPOSURE, HUMIDITY, AND TEMPERATURE 70

HUMIDITY 71
TEMPERATURE 72

CHAPTER 9: THE MANAGEMENT OF INDOOR BONSAI: ARTIFICIAL LIGHTS AND FANS FOR AIR CIRCULATION 74

HOW TO GROW BONSAI INDOORS 74
USE OF ARTIFICIAL LIGHTS FOR BONSAI 75
HOW TO MANAGE AIR CIRCULATION 76

  Overheating protection 77

CHAPTER 10: PREPARING FOR SHOWS AND EXHIBITS: SHOWING AND EVALUATING 79

  How to prepare bonsai for exhibitions 80

  The bonsai exhibition 81

  How bonsai is rated at exhibitions 82

  Participation in exhibitions 83

CHAPTER 11: THE FUTURE OF YOUR BONSAI: MAINTENANCE, IMPROVEMENT, AND PASSION FOR BONSAI 85

  The daily maintenance of the Bonsai 85

  Soil moisture control 86

  Periodic fertilization 87

  Growth and shape tracking 89

  Regular cleaning of the environment 90

  Removal of the Bonsai, if necessary 91

  How to improve your Bonsai 92

  The passion for Bonsai 93

  The future of your Bonsai 95

CONCLUSIONS 97

APPENDIX 1 99

APPENDIX 2 100

APPENDIX 3 101

SUPPORT MY WORK 102

Lucinda Hickman

HI! I'm Lucinda, and I'm thrilled to tell you my story and how I discovered the world of bonsai.

Since childhood, I have always loved nature and spent many hours outdoors among the plants in my garden. Growing up, I became more and more passionate about plant care, and one day, I discovered bonsai. I immediately fell in love with these small trees, their elegant shapes, and their ability to convey serenity.

My passion for bonsai intensified when I visited Japan. I saw how devoted people cared for these plants painstakingly and passionately. So, I decided to learn more and started learning by participating in online seminars and traveling the world to meet and learn from other enthusiasts.

Thanks to my passion and dedication, I have invested many years in becoming a bonsai expert. First, I studied the pruning, fertilizing, and watering techniques needed to grow and keep them healthy. My experience has allowed me to learn from my mistakes and to understand the specific needs of each type of bonsai.

I am proud to have shared my knowledge through the book I wrote. In this text, I have detailed the basic techniques for growing bonsai trees for beginners to help develop and keep them healthy.

My goal is for more and more people to appreciate the beauty of bonsai and the importance of taking care of nature. Furthermore, my book will inspire many more enthusiasts to cultivate bonsai and discover the serenity that only nature can offer.

If you are interested in understanding more about the world of bonsai and staying up to date on future updates, please visit our website, myellowgarden.com, as well as a sponsor of this book and download bonus I prepared for you by framing the QR code.

Finally, I would love to hear your honest opinion by leaving a review on Amazon.

Chapter 1: Introduction. The world of Bonsai

Bonsai are miniature trees grown in specially designed containers to create the feel of an old, mature tree in nature. Growing a bonsai requires a lot of patience, dedication, and a broad knowledge of the botanical world. However, practicing Bonsai can be an advantageous passion and, at the same time, an opportunity to appreciate the nature and beauty of Japanese art.

Bonsai cultivation is an ancient practice that originated in China, where Buddhist monks cultivated miniaturizations of plants as a form of meditation and reflection. The course then spread to Japan, where Bonsai was central to Japanese culture and Zen philosophy. Over time, bonsai cultivation techniques have become increasingly sophisticated and complex, thanks to the research and experimentation of growers worldwide. Today, Bonsai is a living art form expressing nature's beauty worldwide.

Bonsai represents the art of balance between man and nature, where the cultivation and modeling of the Bonsai is a process of cooperation and interaction with the plant itself. Bonsai philosophy in Japan is based on Zen culture, which encourages contemplation and understanding of nature, simplicity, and harmony. This philosophy was adopted in the West. Bonsai was considered an art in which nature is exalted, and man's hand serves its beauty and integrity.

The bonsai cultivation process requires a lot of attention and care. Still, at the same time, it requires respecting the nature of the plant and letting it grow naturally without excessive human interference. In this way, Bonsai becomes an art form in which the artist (the grower) must collaborate with nature rather than dominate it.

Bonsai is, therefore, a practice that encourages patience, concentration, and awareness. Each step in the cultivation process represents a new challenge and an opportunity to learn about nature and oneself.

Bonsai is a highly regarded art form in Japan with ancient roots in Japanese landscape culture and Zen philosophy. Bonsai is viewed as a living work of art that requires a lot of care and patience to cultivate. Bonsai culture in Japan is characterized by ceremonies, exhibitions, and competitions, where bonsai growers present their works to be evaluated by experts in the sector.

In the West, the culture of Bonsai has become increasingly popular since the mid-twentieth century, thanks to the diffusion of specialized books and magazines and to the birth of associations and clubs of bonsai enthusiasts. Today, Bonsai is grown worldwide, and bonsai culture has become a bridge between Japanese and Western culture. This practice combines art and nature uniquely and fascinatingly.

The culture of Bonsai has been influenced by local traditions and each country's climatic and environmental needs. This has led to many bonsai styles, known as bonsai "schools," which have developed specific techniques and philosophies for growing Bonsai. In this way, Bonsai has evolved as a universal art form, capable of connecting different cultures and uniquely expressing the beauty of nature.

Chapter 2: The Choice of Bonsai

The choice of bonsai is one of the first fundamental steps for beginners who want to approach this ancient Japanese practice. There are many factors to consider when choosing a bonsai, such as the species of the tree, its size, and the type of container it is grown in. In this chapter, we will see how to make the right choice for your needs to grow your bonsai tree successfully.

There are many species of bonsai trees, each with its own characteristics and growing requirements. In general, bonsai tree species can be divided into two categories: deciduous species and perennial leaf species.

Deciduous species, such as beech, apple, cherry, and maple, shed their leaves in the fall and are more suited to regions with cold winters. These species are generally less fussy and easier to grow than the perennial leafy species.

Perennial leafy species, such as pines, cypresses, and focuses, retain their leaves throughout the year and are best suited to regions with mild to warm winters. These species require greater control of environmental temperature and humidity to survive.

In addition to choosing the tree species, it is essential to consider the size of the bonsai and the type of container it is grown in. Bonsai can be grown in ceramic, wooden, or plastic pots or in unusual containers such as rocks or hollow logs. Choosing the correct container depends on the species of tree and the size of the bonsai, as well as the desired aesthetic.

Choosing the suitable bonsai, therefore, requires a good knowledge of the various bonsai tree species, their characteristics, and their cultivation requirements. With the right choice, bonsai can become a rewarding art form and a passion for many years.

Bonsai trees come in a wide range of sizes, from miniatures to large specimens that can reach over a meter tall. The bonsai size is essential for its aesthetic presentation and the type of container used. Generally, smaller-sized bonsai trees are more suitable for growing indoors or creating an indoor garden. In contrast, more giant bonsai trees are better suited for growing outdoors or creating an indoor bonsai garden. Bonsai garden in an outdoor area.

Bonsai sizes can be divided into four main categories:

1. **Keshitsubo**: This category includes the most miniature bonsai, which can be grown in tiny pots. These bonsai trees are generally used as art objects to be displayed on a table or desk.
2. **Shito**: This category includes medium-sized bonsai, which can be grown in larger pots than Keshitsubo. These bonsai are suitable for indoor cultivation and for creating a garden in a limited area.

3. **Omono**: this category includes large bonsai, which can be grown in large pots or directly in the ground. These bonsai are suitable for growing outdoors or creating a garden outdoors.
4. **Imperial**: this category includes bonsai of monumental dimensions, which require large spaces for their cultivation and presentation. These bonsai

are generally found in public parks or extensive botanical gardens.

The choice of the size of the bonsai depends on the aesthetic needs of the grower and on the size of the area available for its cultivation. The bonsai size can also create a particular atmosphere; for example, a large bonsai can be used as a focal point in a zen garden, while a small bonsai can develop a feeling of harmony and tranquility indoors. Home interior.

Materials for growing bonsai

In addition to the choice of tree species and the bonsai size, it is also essential to consider the materials used for cultivation. The materials used for growing bonsai include pots, soil, substrates, and fertilizers.

Bonsai pots can be made of ceramic, wood, plastic, or terracotta. The choice of pot material depends on the aesthetic needs of the grower and the needs of the bonsai tree species. For example, ceramics and wood are often preferred for their beauty and breathing ability but require more attention when watering and maintaining. Plastic and terracotta pots, on the other hand, are easier to manage but can be less aesthetic.

The land for bonsai must be chosen carefully to ensure the proper growth of the plant. In addition, the ground for the bonsai must be well drained and aerated to ensure adequate circulation of air and water around the roots of the plant. Bonsai soil can be purchased ready-made or prepared manually by mixing different types of soil and specific substrates for bonsai.

Substrates for bonsai include gravel, sand, moss, and other materials, which are used to create the desired effect around the bonsai roots. The substrates for the bonsai are chosen according to the needs of the bonsai tree species and the aesthetic needs of the grower.

Finally, fertilizers for bonsai are essential to ensure the proper growth of the plant. Fertilizers for bonsai must be chosen according to the specific needs of the bonsai tree species. In addition, they must be used carefully to avoid burning the plant's roots.

Choosing suitable materials for growing bonsai is, therefore, a vital operation to ensure the healthy and vigorous growth of the plant. With the proper attention and care, bonsai can become a source of beauty and inspiration for many years.

The choice of bonsai depends not only on the plant's needs but also on the grower's needs. Bonsai requires a lot of attention and care. Therefore, choosing a suitable bonsai depends on the grower's time, space, and resource availability.

If the grower is short on time, he can choose a bonsai that requires less maintenance, such as a small-sized bonsai or a tree species that requires less pruning. In this way, the grower can enjoy bonsai's benefits without spending too much time cultivating it.

If the grower has limited space, he can opt for a small-sized bonsai, or one grown in small-sized pots. This way, the grower can grow the bonsai indoors or in a limited outdoor area without taking up too much space.

If the grower has limited resources, he may choose a bonsai that requires less attention and fewer resources, such as a tree species that grows well in its climatic zone or a bonsai that requires less fertilizer and more occasional substrate changes.

In any case, choosing the suitable bonsai depends on the needs and preferences of the grower. It requires a good knowledge of the bonsai tree species, their characteristics, and their cultivation requirements. With the right choice, bonsai can become a source of beauty, inspiration, and personal gratification for many years.

Chapter 3: The basics of Bonsai

To grow a healthy and robust bonsai, it is essential to know the basics, which include choosing suitable soil, proper watering, fertilizing, and pruning. In this chapter, we will look at every aspect of the bonsai cultivation process to ensure the healthy and vigorous growth of the plant.

The ideal land for bonsai: Types, Properties, and Preparation

Bonsai soil must be chosen carefully to ensure proper air and water circulation around the plant's roots. The earth for the bonsai must be well-drained to avoid water stagnation around the bases. It must be rich in nutrients to ensure healthy and vigorous growth of the plant.

Types of soil for bonsai include pre-packed earth, manually prepared earth, and substrates. Pre-packed soil is available at garden supply stores. It combines soil, sand, and other materials to ensure proper drainage and aeration around the bonsai's roots. On the other hand, the grower prepares the earth manually, mixing different types of soil and specific substrates for the bonsai. Substrates include gravel, sand, moss, and other materials used to create the desired effect around the bonsai roots.

The properties of the earth for bonsai include porosity, the ability to hold moisture, and the ability to provide nutrients to the plant. Good soil for bonsai must have adequate porosity to ensure proper air and water circulation around the plant's roots. The ground for the bonsai must also retain moisture for a sufficient period to avoid dehydration of the plant. Finally, the earth for bonsai must be able to supply nutrients to the plant, such as nitrogen, phosphorus, and potassium.

To prepare the soil for bonsai, it is essential to mix the different soil types and substrates evenly to ensure proper air and water circulation around the plant's roots. Preparing the land for bonsai requires a lot of attention and care, but it is a crucial step to ensure the healthy and vigorous growth of the plant.

Bonsai watering: when and how to water

Watering is one of the most important aspects of bonsai cultivation, as the amount and frequency of watering affect the health and growth of the plant. The bonsai needs water to grow, but it is important not to overwater the plant. Otherwise, the roots could rot, and the plant could die.

To determine how often and how much to water your bonsai, it is crucial to consider several factors, such as the type of tree species, the size of the pot, the temperature and humidity of the surrounding environment, and the season of the year.

Generally, the bonsai must be watered when the soil dries out slightly on the surface. However, it is essential to water. Otherwise, the plant roots could be damaged. On the other hand, it is necessary not to flood the bonsai excessively, as too wet soil can cause root rot.

The watering method depends on the size and location of the bonsai. For small bonsai, watering can be done by immersing the pot in a water container for a few minutes to allow the earth to absorb the excess water. For large bonsai, watering can be done using a garden hose or drip irrigation.

It is also essential to ensure that the water does not contain chlorine or other chemicals, as they can damage the bonsai roots. Furthermore, it is important not to water the bonsai during the hottest hours of the day, as the water deposited on the leaves could burn them.

In summary, watering bonsai requires attention and care. Still, with the proper practice and knowledge, the grower can ensure healthy and vigorous plant growth.

Fertilization of bonsai: frequency, types, and doses

Fertilizing is a fundamental aspect of bonsai cultivation, as bonsai need good nutrients to grow healthily and vigorously. Fertilizing helps give the plant the nutrients it needs for growth, including nitrogen, phosphorus, and potassium.

The frequency of fertilizing depends on the tree species, the season of the year, and the type of fertilizer used. Generally, bonsai requires fertilization during active growth, which usually corresponds to spring and summer. However, the bonsai requires lighter or no fertilization during the winter dormancy.

There are different types of fertilizers for bonsai, including organic fertilizers and inorganic fertilizers. Organic fertilizers, such as manure and compost, are natural and provide nutrients to the plant over the long term. Inorganic fertilizers, such as slow-release fertilizers and water-soluble fertilizers, give nutrients to the plant quickly and accurately.

The fertilizer dose depends on the tree species and the fertilizer type used. Generally, following the manufacturer's directions regarding the amount and frequency of fertilizing is essential. Also, avoiding using too much fertilizer is important, as it can burn the plant's roots.

In summary, bonsai fertilization is an essential aspect of bonsai cultivation, requiring attention and care to ensure the healthy and vigorous growth of the plant. The choice of the type of fertilizer and its application depends on the tree species, the season of the year, and the plant's specific needs.

Bonsai pruning cutting and modeling techniques

Pruning is a vital bonsai cultivation technique. It consists of cutting certain tree parts to control its growth and shape. Pruning helps maintain the desired shape of the bonsai, promotes branching, and removes any diseased or damaged parts of the tree.

There are two main types of pruning: training pruning and maintenance pruning. Training pruning is done when the bonsai is still young and is intended to shape the tree's shape. Maintenance pruning, on the other hand, is carried out on mature trees and aims to maintain the desired shape of the tree and control its growth.

Trimming techniques include flush trimming, overflow trimming, and thinning trimming. The flush cut is done by cutting the branch flush with the bark, while the overflow cut is done by cutting the branch slightly above a node. The thinning amount is made by removing an entire unit. In contrast, the thinning cut is made by removing some smaller branches.

Modeling is another important bonsai cultivation technique, which involves modeling the tree's shape through pruning and removing unwanted parts of the tree. Modeling takes time and patience but can produce spectacular results.

For pruning and shaping bonsai, it is essential to use specific tools, such as bonsai shears, branch ashlars, and leaf shears. It is also necessary to keep the tools clean and sharp to avoid damage to the plant.

Pruning and shaping are essential bonsai growing techniques that require knowledge and practice. However, with the proper design and tools, the grower can ensure healthy and vigorous bonsai growth and achieve spectacular results.

Chapter 4: Transplantation

Transplanting is a vital bonsai cultivation operation. It consists of removing the plant from the pot and transplanting it into a new pot with new soil. Transplanting allows the bonsai roots to grow in a new environment, ensuring a better circulation of air and water around the roots and a better supply of nutrients to the plant. In this chapter, we will look at the bonsai transplanting process, from choosing the right time for transplanting to preparing the bonsai for transplanting.

When is the right time to transplant a bonsai?

The right time for transplanting depends on the tree species and the plant's specific needs. Generally, bonsai transplantation is done every 2-3 years for young bonsai trees, while older bonsai trees may need to be transplanted every 4-5 years. It is essential to avoid transplanting the bonsai during the rest season, as the plant could suffer excessive damage.

Some pointers can help determine the right time for transplanting your bonsai. For example, if the bonsai roots begin to protrude from the bottom of the pot or the soil starts to become compact and rugged, it's time to transplant the bonsai. Also, if the plant doesn't seem to grow or the foliage turns yellow or brown, the bonsai may need to be transplanted.

The best time to transplant bonsai is during spring when the plant grows actively. When transplanting, it is essential to carefully remove the plant from the old pot and remove any dead or damaged roots. Subsequently, the plant is transplanted into a new pot with new soil and fertilized to stimulate growth.

In summary, bonsai transplanting is an essential bonsai cultivation operation, which requires knowledge and practice to be carried out correctly. The right time for transplanting depends on the tree species and the plant's specific needs. Still, transplanting is generally done every 2-3 years for young bonsai.

How to prepare bonsai for transplanting

Before transplanting the bonsai, preparing the plant for the change is essential. Preparation includes several operations, including pruning the roots, removing old soil, and pruning the plant.

Root pruning is an essential operation that removes dead or damaged roots and promotes new root growth. For the pruning of the sources, a bonsai rake or a sharp knife can be used, cutting off the excess seeds and keeping only the healthiest and most vital ones. It is recommended not to remove more than 30% of the roots when transplanting, to avoid excessive damage to the plant.

Next, the old soil around the roots of the bonsai is removed. A bonsai rake or knife can carefully remove the dirt around the bases. It is essential to avoid damaging the roots during this operation to ensure the plant's health.

Finally, you can proceed with the pruning of the plant, which consists of cutting off unwanted parts of the tree to control the growth and shape of the plant. Pruning the plant can be done at the same time as pruning the roots, as both operations require the removal of unwanted parts of the tree.

Once the plant has been prepared for transplanting, the bonsai can be removed from the old pot and transplanted into a new pot with fresh soil. When transplanting, it is essential to handle the plant carefully, to avoid damaging the roots or the plant itself.

In summary, preparing bonsai for transplanting is a critical operation that requires knowledge and practice to be carried out correctly. Preparation includes pruning the roots, removing old soil, and pruning the plant. Once the plant has been prepared, the bonsai can be removed from the old pot and transplanted into a new pot with new soil.

The transplant technique: step by step

The bonsai transplant technique requires attention and care, as the plant could be damaged if the method is not carried out correctly. Here is a step-by-step guide for transplanting bonsai:

1. Prepare the new pot and new soil: choose the right size and prepare the new earth with the proper substrates and fertilizers for the tree species.
2. Prepare the bonsai for transplanting: remove the plant from the old pot and the old soil from the roots. Prune the seeds and plant as needed.
3. Place the bonsai in the new pot: Insert it into the unique pot and place it in the pool's center. Fill the pot with fresh soil and compact the ground around the bonsai roots.
4. Irrigate the bonsai: Irrigate the bonsai with clean water so that the new earth adheres well to the bonsai's roots. Remove any air bubbles from the world.

5. Add Fertilizer: Add as much fertilizer as needed to the new land, based on the tree species and the year's season.
6. Place the bonsai in shelter: place the bonsai away from the sun and wind for a few days to allow the plant to recover from the transplant.
7. When transplanting the bonsai, it is essential to avoid damaging the plant's roots and to handle the plant carefully. It is also necessary to use the new earth and fertilizers suitable for the tree species to ensure the plant's health.

The bonsai transplant technique requires attention and care to be carried out correctly. However, by following the correct procedure, it is possible to transplant the bonsai safely and ensure the healthy and vigorous growth of the plant.

Post-transplant care: watering, fertilizing, and rest

After transplanting the bonsai, it is essential to provide the plant with the proper care to ensure healthy and vigorous growth. Post-transplant care includes watering, fertilizing, and rest.

Irrigation is essential to maintain the correct humidity of the soil around the roots of the bonsai. Therefore, during the first days after transplanting, it is necessary to irrigate the bonsai with clean water and keep it away from the sun and wind. Subsequently, watering can be done according to the specific needs of the tree species.

Fertilizing is another vital operation to provide the plant with the nutrients necessary for growth. Therefore, during the first months after transplanting, it is advisable to use specific fertilizers for the post-transplant period to stimulate root growth and plant recovery. Subsequently, the fertilizer for the tree species and according to the year's season can be used.

Rest is an important phase of recovery for bonsai after transplanting. During the first days after transplanting, keeping the bonsai away from the sun and the wind is advisable to allow the plant to adapt to the new situation. In general, it is advisable to avoid handling the plant during the post-transplant rest period, to avoid damaging the plant.

Post-transplant care for bonsai includes watering, fertilizing, and resting. Providing the plant with the proper care after transplanting is essential to ensure healthy and vigorous growth of the plant.

Chapter 5: Building the Trunk: techniques of Wire, weaving, and Bandaging.

Forming the bonsai trunk is vital to creating a natural and harmonious-looking plant. The position and angle of the box are two fundamental elements in the formation of bonsai, as they influence the plant's general appearance. In this chapter, we will examine how to choose the position and angle of the bonsai trunk to create a natural and harmonious-looking plant.

How to choose the position and angle of the trunk

The position and angle of the trunk are fundamental elements in modeling the bonsai, as they determine the balance and harmony of the tree. When choosing the location and angle of the box, it is essential to consider the tree species, its natural growth style, and the desired aesthetic effect.

Regarding the position, the bonsai's trunk can be oriented in various directions, such as forwards, backward, to the right, or left. However, the part of the trunk must be chosen to create a feeling of balance and movement. For this reason, it is essential to observe the plant carefully and evaluate which position best suits its natural growth style.

The angle of the trunk, on the other hand, determines the visual effect of the tree and can be used to create a feeling of stability or movement. For example, a leaning torso can make the impression of motion. In contrast, an upright torso can give peace and solidity.

Bonsai trunk angle refers to the trunk's lean or curvature relative to the tree's base. This is an essential element in bonsai modeling as it determines the tree's visual effect and overall balance. For example, an inclined torso can create a sense of movement. In contrast, an upright torso can give a sense of stability and solidity. The angle of the trunk can be achieved by using the copper wire to bend the box to create the desired shape. In summary, the bonsai trunk angle refers to the curvature or lean of the trunk. It can be used to create any desired aesthetic effect.

To choose the position and angle of the trunk, it is helpful to use the copper wire to shape the plant to create the desired shape. It is also essential to consider the overall aesthetic effect of the tree, and not just the shape of the trunk but also the shape and arrangement of the branches and crown.

In general, choose a trunk position and angle that reflects the tree's natural beauty and creates a feeling of balance and harmony. Of course, selecting the location and angle of the trunk can take some practice and experimentation. Still, a stunning trunk bonsai can be created with the proper care and dedication.

Wire techniques: how to shape the trunk with copper wire.

The copper wire technique is one of the most used techniques to shape the bonsai trunk. The copper wire is soft and pliable, allowing you to shape the compartment into the desired position and angle. Here are the steps to use the copper wire technique to shape the trunk of the bonsai:

1. Choosing the copper wire: The copper wire must be the right size for the bonsai trunk and must not damage the bark. It is recommended to use soft and flexible copper wires to avoid damaging the plant's bark.
2. Apply the copper wire: Wrap the copper wire around the trunk of the bonsai at the desired position and angle. Ensure the copper wire is wrapped tightly around the box without crushing the plant's bark.
3. Shape the trunk: Shape the bonsai's box to the desired position and angle, using the copper wire as a guide. Again, ensure not to force the plant or damage the roots or leaves.
4. Remove the copper wire: After a few weeks or months, the copper wire can be removed from the bonsai trunk once the plant has taken up the desired position. Removing the copper wire carefully is essential to avoid damaging the plant's bark.

The copper wire technique is effective for shaping the bonsai's trunk into the desired position and angle.

However, it is essential to use copper wire carefully to avoid damaging the plant's bark and ensure healthy and vigorous plant growth.

The copper wire technique is one of the most used techniques to shape the bonsai trunk. Using the copper wire correctly, you can shape the box into the desired position and angle, creating a harmonious and natural-looking plant.

Weaving techniques: how to shape the trunk by intertwining the branches.

Braiding techniques vary from the copper wire technique for shaping the bonsai trunk. This technique involves twisting the plant's components, creating a natural and harmonious-looking bin. Here are the steps to use the braiding process to shape the trunk of the bonsai:

- Choose the branches: choose the plant's branches to intertwine to create a solid and harmonious structure. It is advisable to use young and flexible components to facilitate interweaving.
- Intertwining the branches: interweaving the plant's stems, creating a solid and harmonious structure.

Ensure the components are tightly intertwined without crushing the plant's bark or damaging the leaves.
- Shape the trunk: shape the bonsai's trunk using the intertwined branches as a guide. Make sure not to force the plant or damage the roots or leaves.
- Monitor growth: Monitor plant growth to prevent intertwined branches from becoming damaged or causing damage to the plant. If necessary, some of the intertwined branches can be removed to ensure the healthy and vigorous growth of the plant.

Braiding techniques are effective for shaping the bonsai's trunk into the desired position and angle. However, it is essential to use the branches with care to avoid damaging the plant's bark and ensure healthy and vigorous plant growth.

Braiding techniques vary from the copper wire technique for shaping the bonsai trunk. However, adequately intertwined branches can shape the compartment into the desired position and angle, creating a harmonious and natural-looking plant.

Bandaging techniques: how to shape the trunk by bending it.

Bandaging is one of the techniques used in modeling the bonsai trunk. This technique consists in turning the box into a desired position and maintaining this position with the help of a bandage or elastic tape. Depending on the desired aesthetic effect, the application creates smooth curves or sharp angles in the trunk.

To use this technique correctly, it is essential to choose the right moment when the bonsai trunk is flexible enough to bend but not so rigid that it breaks. In general, spring or summer are the best times to wrap.

Before bending the trunk, it is necessary to prepare it with the help of copper wire, which will make it more flexible and ready for turning. Once the box has been placed in the desired position, it must be secured with a bandage or elastic tape to keep it in place until it has acquired a stable shape.

It is essential to constantly monitor the trunk during bandaging, ensuring it does not crack or suffer damage. Once the desired shape has been achieved, the bandage or elastic tape can be removed, but the trunk must be held in this position for some time to gain stability.

When monitoring the trunk, you should check the bonsai trunk regularly to ensure it does not suffer damage or crack during the bending process. During the bandaging period, the bonsai's box can experience considerable stress, so it is essential to check it frequently to avoid damage or cracking. Monitoring the trunk at least once a day is recommended, especially in the first days after bending. In the event of problems or signs of stress, it is essential to take immediate action to avoid further damage.

Constant trunk monitoring during the bandaging period requires some attention and care. Still, it is crucial to ensure that the bonsai remains healthy and in good condition.

Chapter 6: Canopy Formation: leaf cutting, green pruning, and Defoliation.

The shape and size of the crown are two fundamental elements for creating a harmonious and natural-looking bonsai. The choice of the body and height size depends on the plant's characteristics, the style of bonsai to be made, and the grower's experience. Here are some tips for choosing the shape and size of the bonsai canopy:

- Choosing the style of bonsai: choose the style of bonsai you want to create based on the shape and size of the plant. There are different bonsai styles, such as formal, informal, cascading, and windswept bonsai.
- Observe the plant: observe it carefully to identify its natural shape and distinctive characteristics. This will help determine the shape and size of the crown.
- Choose the main branches: choose the main branches of the plant to create a solid and harmonious structure. Ensure the components are well-spaced and distributed on the canopy.
- Modeling the canopy: modeling the bonsai canopy using leaf-cutting, green pruning, and Defoliation. These techniques allow you to model the foliage in the desired shape and size, eliminating unwanted parts of the plant.

The choice of the crown's shape and size depends on the plant's characteristics, the style of bonsai to be created, and the grower's experience. Therefore, observing the plant carefully and shaping the crown gradually is essential to create a harmonious and natural-looking bonsai.

The shape and size of the crown are two fundamental elements for creating a harmonious and natural-looking bonsai. Using the techniques of leaf trimming, green pruning, and Defoliation, it is possible to shape the crown of the bonsai into the desired shape and size, creating a harmonious and natural-looking plant.

Leaf-cutting techniques: how to shape the foliage by cutting the leaves.

Leaf trimming is a very versatile modeling technique, as it can be used to shape the bonsai canopy's general shape, reduce the leaves' size, or emphasize specific bonsai lines or features.

Trimming the leaves is more effective for creating a thicker, denser canopy. This is particularly useful for bonsai species with too "open" ceilings or needing more branching. Reducing the number of leaves can also encourage the production of new shoots, stimulating the growth of fresh leaves and new branches.

As for the leaf-trimming process, it is essential to remember that the leaves are the bonsai's primary energy source, so trimming too many leaves can cause excessive stress. It is, therefore, necessary to limit the number of leaves cut at a time and not to cut too close to the main branch. Otherwise, you risk damaging the bonsai and slowing down its growth.

In general, it is advisable to cut the leaves during the growing season of the bonsai, when its metabolism is most active. This way, the bonsai has more energy to recover from the cut and to produce new leaves.

Leaf trimming is an essential technique for modeling the shape and density of the bonsai canopy. With the proper knowledge and attention, this technique can achieve stunning results without damaging the bonsai.

For example, if the bonsai canopy is too tall or too wide about the trunk, leaf trimming can reduce its size. In addition, a more compact and harmonious shape can be created by trimming the leaves along the outer edge of the canopy. Alternatively, suppose the bonsai has an irregular shape. In that case, leaf trimming can emphasize specific lines or features of the bonsai.

Also, leaf trimming can be used to increase canopy density. For example, suppose the bonsai canopy has few branches or is too open. In that case, some leaves can be cut along the stems, encouraging branching and the production of new shoots.

Of course, cutting only a few leaves at a time is essential. Excessive cutting can damage the bonsai and reduce its ability to photosynthesize. Also, leaf trimming should be one of many techniques used to shape the shape of the bonsai. Pruning the branches and cutting the roots is essential to creating a harmonious and balanced body.

Green pruning techniques

Green pruning is a technique for shaping a bonsai crown, which consists of pruning the components of the plant to obtain the desired shape and size. This technique is mainly used for large-leaved plants, such as figs or junipers. Here are the steps to use the green pruning technique to shape the bonsai canopy:

Choosing the branches to prune choose the branches of the plant based on the shape and size of the desired crown. It is recommended to prune larger branches and branches in the wrong places in the canopy.

Use scissors: Use scissors to prune the branches of the plant. It is advisable to prune the branches gradually to avoid damaging the plant.

Monitor growth: monitor the development of the plant to prevent the green pruning technique from damaging the plant or limiting its growth.

Shaping the canopy: Shaping the top of the bonsai using the green pruning technique as a guide. Ensure you prune the branches sparingly or damage the plant's vital parts.

The green pruning technique effectively shapes the bonsai canopy into the desired shape and size. However, it is essential to use the shears with care to avoid damaging the plant and ensure healthy and vigorous plant growth.

Green pruning is a technique for shaping a bonsai crown, which consists of pruning the branches of the plant to obtain the desired shape and size. Using the scissors correctly, it is possible to shape the crown of the bonsai naturally and harmoniously.

Defoliation: when and how to defoliate the bonsai

Defoliation is an advanced bonsai crown modeling technique that consists of the complete removal of the leaves of the tree. This technique can be used to restructure the bonsai canopy or reduce the size of the leaves. Still, it should be done cautiously as it can be stressful for the bonsai.

Generally, Defoliation is done once a year, usually in the summer when the bonsai is in total growth. This period is ideal for Defoliation as it allows the tree to develop new leaves by the end of the season.

Before proceeding with Defoliation, it is essential to consider the bonsai's health and its specific needs. For example, deciduous trees such as beech, maple, or linden are ideal for Defoliation. In contrast, perennial trees such as pine or conifer should not be defoliated, as this can cause irreparable damage to them.

To perform Defoliation, all leaves must be removed from the tree. This can be done manually or with a clean pair of scissors. However, it is essential to avoid cutting the small shoots near the base of the leaves, as they are necessary for the future growth of the bonsai.

Once the leaves have been removed, the bonsai should be kept in the shade and moist for a few days. This is because Defoliation can cause water stress on the bonsai as the number of leaves that absorb water decreases. After about two weeks, the bonsai should produce new leaves.

Also, it is essential to avoid defoliating during stress for the bonsai, such as during flowering or fruiting. Also, the bonsai has been defoliated in the past. In that case, waiting at least two to three years before defoliating it again is essential, as repeated practice can weaken the tree.

Defoliation is an advanced bonsai canopy modeling technique that can be beneficial when done correctly. However, it should be done with caution and only on solid and healthy trees, considering the species of tree and its specific needs.

Chapter 7: Disease and Pest Management: Prevention and Natural Remedies

The management of diseases and pests: prevention and natural remedies

The health of the bonsai is essential to its beauty and longevity. Unfortunately, Bonsai trees are subject to various diseases and pests, which can compromise their health. Therefore, it's necessary to take the proper precautions to prevent illness and problems and be prepared to intervene when necessary. This chapter will explore the significant bonsai diseases and pests and how to manage them naturally and sustainably.

The primary diseases of bonsai and how to prevent them.

Bonsai diseases can be caused by many factors, including climatic conditions, nutrient deficiencies, excessive exposure to sun or shade, and overwatering or underwatering. Here are some of the significant bonsai diseases and how to prevent them:

- Root rot: Root rot is a disease caused by too much water or too heavy soil. To prevent root rot, make sure you use a well-draining substrate and don't overwater.
- White mold: White mold is a disease caused by excessive humidity and too low temperatures. To prevent white mold, avoid wetting the leaves and overwatering them.

- Anthracnose: anthracnose is a disease caused by a fungus that attacks the leaves and fruits of the bonsai. To prevent anthracnose, avoid overwatering and wetting the leaves.
- Fig leaf disease: Fig leaf disease is caused by a fungus that attacks the leaves of the fig tree. To prevent fig leaf disease, avoid overwatering and wetting the leaves.
- To prevent bonsai diseases, it is essential to keep the plant healthy and vigorous, avoid excess water and humidity, and provide the plant with the nutrients it needs.

The main bonsai pests and how to prevent them.

Pests are another threat to bonsai health. They can be carried by winds, insects, or garden visitors and infect plants quickly. Here are some of the main bonsai pests and how to prevent them:

- Mites: mites are tiny insects that suck the sap of plants, causing yellow leaves and early falls. To prevent spider mites, avoid wetting the leaves and keep the garden clean.

- Aphids: aphids are tiny insects that suck the sap of plants, causing the deformation of leaves and foliage. To prevent aphids, avoid overwatering and keep your garden clean.
- Cochineal: the cochineal is a tiny insect that attaches itself to the leaves and roots of plants, causing damage and deformation. To prevent mealybugs, avoid wetting the leaves and keep the garden clean.
- Nematodes: nematodes are worms that attack the roots of plants, causing damage and deformation. To prevent nematodes, use a quality substrate and keep the plant healthy and vigorous.

To prevent bonsai pests, it is essential to keep the garden clean and to use natural methods of prevention, such as using repulsive plants, such as mint, garlic, and basil, and using vegetable oils for insect control. In the event of an infestation, natural products based on neem oil or Marseille soap can be used to remove the parasites without harming the plant.

Natural remedies for bonsai diseases and pests

There are several natural remedies to manage bonsai diseases and pests. Here are some examples:

Neem oil

Neem oil is a very effective natural remedy for preventing and treating many diseases and pests that can affect bonsai trees. It is extracted from the seeds of the neem tree, a plant native to India and widely used in Ayurvedic medicine.

Neem oil contains azadirachtin, an active ingredient that acts as a natural insecticide, repelling insects that attack bonsai trees. Furthermore, it has antifungal and antibacterial properties, making it effective against fungal and bacterial diseases.

To use neem oil on your bonsai, you can dilute it in water (1-2 tablespoons of oil per liter of water) and spray it on the leaves and branches or apply it directly on the parts affected by disease or insects. In general, it is essential to pay attention to the amount of neem oil used to avoid damaging the health of the bonsai.

Neem oil is a beneficial natural remedy for preventing and treating many bonsai problems. However, it is essential to remember that, as with all natural remedies, results may vary depending on the type of bonsai and the extent of disease or pest attack. When in doubt, it is always best to seek advice from an expert.

Garlic

Garlic is a common natural remedy for preventing and treating many bonsai diseases. It contains allicin, which has antifungal, antibacterial, and antiviral properties.

To use garlic on your bonsai, prepare a homemade spray solution: crush some garlic cloves and let them soak in water for a few hours. After filtering the solution, spray it on the leaves and branches of the bonsai.

Alternatively, you can plant garlic around your bonsai to create an area protected from disease and pests.

However, it is essential to keep in mind that garlic can also have adverse effects on the bonsai's health if not used correctly or in excessive quantities. Furthermore, not all bonsai can tolerate the smell of garlic, so it is always advisable to test it on a small portion of the plant before using it on the entire surface of the bonsai.

Water and soap

Soap and water are other effective natural remedies for eliminating parasites on bonsai trees. In addition, this method is beneficial for combating visible pests such as spider mites and aphids.

To use soap and water, mix a few tablespoons of natural liquid soap or dish soap into a gallon of warm water. Then, dip a soft cloth or sponge into the solution and gently wipe the leaves and branches of the bonsai, making sure to cover all affected surfaces.

Afterward, rinse the bonsai with clean water and dry it carefully. Repeat this once a week until the parasites are eliminated.

It is essential to pay attention to the concentration of soap used: too strong a solution could damage the bonsai, while too weak a resolution may not be enough to eliminate parasites. In general, a 2% soap solution is adequate for most parasites.

Furthermore, it is essential to avoid using soap on particularly sensitive bonsai or under stress, as it could further damage them. Finally, it is always advisable to test the product on a small area of the bonsai before using it on the whole plant.

Nettle

Nettle has numerous beneficial properties, including as a natural repellent for bonsai parasites. In addition, nettles contain chemical compounds that can help keep aphids, thrips, and spider mites away.

To use nettle as a repellent, you can prepare an infusion using the fresh or dried leaves of the plant. To do this, fill a container with water and add about 100 grams of nettle leaves for every liter. Let the mixture sit for 24-48 hours, then strain the liquid and spray it on the bonsai, covering all affected surfaces.

The nettle infusion can be used as a prevention against parasites by spraying the bonsai once a week. Alternatively, it can also combat an existing infestation by increasing the frequency of applications.

It is essential to pay attention to the concentration of the infusion: too strong a solution could damage the bonsai, while too weak a resolution could not be effective in keeping parasites away. Generally, a 5-10% solution of nettle leaves is adequate for most pests.

Furthermore, it is essential to be careful not to spray the nettle infusion on the flowers or fruits of the bonsai, as it could alter their flavor. Finally, it is always advisable to test the product on a small area of the bonsai before using it on the whole plant.

Acetic acid more details

Acetic acid, or ethnic acid, is a colorless, pungent-smelling organic acid commonly used as a food preservative and ingredient for making sauces and condiments.

In gardening and bonsai cultivation, acetic acid can be used as a natural remedy to fight fungi and molds. Its fungicidal action derives from the dehydrating and bactericidal effect of the acid on the mushroom spores.

To prepare an acetic acid solution, one part acid can be mixed with 10 parts of water. Then, the answer can be applied to the leaves and soil of the bonsai using a vaporizer. It is essential to pay attention to the concentration of the solution, as too much acid can damage the leaves and roots of the bonsai.

As with all natural remedies, acetic acid should be used cautiously and only if necessary. It is always best to consult an expert or professional gardener when in doubt.

Chamomile

Chamomile is an herbaceous plant with white or yellow flowers belonging to the Asteraceae family. It is best known for its calming and soothing properties. Still, it is also used in gardening and bonsai cultivation as a natural remedy against insects.

To prepare a chamomile solution, dried or fresh flowers can be used. Using 50-60 grams of flowers for each liter of water is recommended. Let the water boil for a few minutes, and then pour the solution into a spray container.

The solution can be sprayed on the canopy of the bonsai to combat insects such as aphids, whiteflies, and scale insects. In addition, chamomile acts as a natural repellent, preventing insects from attacking the bonsai and preventing their proliferation.

Furthermore, chamomile can also be used as a natural fertilizer for bonsai. In fact, thanks to its organic components, chamomile helps fertilize the soil and improve the health of the bonsai roots.

As with all natural remedies, it is essential to use chamomile in moderation and not overdo it to avoid damaging the bonsai. It is always best to consult an expert or professional gardener when in doubt.

Almond oil

Almond oil can be a natural remedy for bonsai care as it contains vital nutrients, such as vitamin E and essential fatty acids, which help maintain plant health. Almond oil can improve the appearance of bonsai leaves, giving them a more glossy and vital appearance.

To use almond oil as a natural remedy for bonsai, simply dilute it in water and spray the solution on the plant leaves. This will help moisturize the leaves and prevent dryness and spots.

Almond oil can also be used as a natural fertilizer for bonsai trees. In this case, you can mix the oil with water and other nourishing ingredients, such as green tea or baking soda, and use the solution to water the plant.

In general, almond oil is a very effective natural remedy for bonsai care, as it is delicate but nourishing and moisturizing at the same time.

Green tea

Green tea can be used as a natural remedy for bonsai care as it contains essential antioxidants and nutrients which help maintain plant health. Green tea can improve the soil quality of bonsai and prevent the formation of fungi or other pathogens.

To use green tea as a natural remedy for bonsai, you can prepare a solution using an infused green tea bag. Once the solution has been prepared, it can be diluted and used to water the bonsai. In this way, green tea will help enrich the bonsai soil with essential nutrients and antioxidants, improving the overall health of the plant.

Alternatively, green tea can also be used as a spray for the bonsai leaves. In this case, it is sufficient to dilute the green tea solution in water and spray it on the bonsai leaves. This will help hydrate and nourish the bonsai leaves, preventing dryness and spots.

In general, green tea is a very effective natural remedy for bonsai care, as it is delicate but at the same time nourishing and rich in antioxidant substances.

Copper

Copper is a natural remedy to fight fungi and rust on bonsai leaves. It can be used as copper sulfate, which is diluted in water and then sprayed on plants. Copper sulfate also has antiparasitic properties, helping prevent insect pest attacks. However, using copper cautiously and only when necessary is essential, as excess copper can be toxic to plants and the surrounding environment. Additionally, copper can stain surfaces and be corrosive when used in large quantities.

Ginger

Ginger is a root also used as a natural remedy for bonsai care. It contains natural antibacterial, antifungal, and antioxidant compounds that can help protect plants from disease and pests. To use ginger as a remedy, you can prepare a solution with grated fresh ginger and warm water. Let the solution sit for a while, and then filter it. Use the key to water the bonsai or spray it on the leaves. Alternatively, a few slices of ginger can be added to the bonsai soil if the roots are already well-developed. However, it is essential to remember that too much ginger can become toxic to the bonsai. Use it in moderation and only when needed.

Aloe vera juice

Aloe vera juice is known for its healing properties and can also be used for bonsai care. It is rich in enzymes, minerals, vitamins, and antioxidant substances that can help strengthen the plant and prevent the onset of diseases and parasites. You can buy a ready-made product or extract the juice from fresh leaves to use aloe vera juice. To do this, cut an aloe vera leaf and remove the hard outer part, leaving only the fine inner pulp. Blend the pulp and filter it with a sieve to remove residues. Use the solution to water the bonsai or spray it on the leaves. Aloe vera juice can also be added to bonsai soil to improve health. However, using only high-quality, pure aloe vera juice is essential, as aloe vera products can contain preservatives and additives that can harm the bonsai.

How to intervene in case of problems

If the bonsai shows symptoms of disease or pest infestation, it is essential to intervene promptly to prevent further damage. Here are some steps to follow in case of problems:

- Identify the problem: look closely at the plant and try to identify the problem. Sometimes, it may be necessary to seek advice from a bonsai expert.
- Take the proper precautions: isolate the bonsai from other plants to prevent the problem from spreading. Wear gloves and a mask to protect the plant and yourself.
- Apply the remedy: evenly apply the chosen natural remedy or chemical product on the plant. Follow the

manufacturer's instructions to avoid damaging the plant.

- Monitor the plant: observe the plant closely over the next few days to see if the problem has been resolved. If not, repeat the treatment or look for other solutions.

In general, it is essential to pay attention to the bonsai's health and to intervene promptly in case of problems. Keeping the plant healthy and vigorous, using natural prevention methods, and swiftly remedying the issues are essential for the longevity and beauty of the bonsai.

Chapter 8: Climate Management: exposure, humidity, and Temperature

The climate is a crucial factor in the health and beauty of bonsai. Good climate management can make the difference between a healthy bonsai and a diseased one. Choosing the correct display for bonsai is one of the most important factors to consider.

To choose the correct exposure, several factors must be considered, including the species of bonsai, the climate of the area, and the surrounding environment. Generally, most bonsai prefer a well-lit location. Still, they are not exposed to direct sunlight to avoid overheating the substrate and roots.

The choice of exposure also depends on the season: in summer, when temperatures are higher, it is advisable to expose the bonsai in a partially shaded position, while in winter, when temperatures are lower, it is advisable to tell the bonsai in a sunnier.

Furthermore, it is essential to consider the humidity of the air and the substrate. Many bonsai prefer a humid environment, so placing it in an area with good air circulation and keeping the substrate moist but not too wet is advisable.

Finally, it is essential to consider the Temperature: most bonsai prefer a moderate temperature, avoiding temperatures that are too high or too low. For this reason, it is advisable to place the bonsai in an area protected from drafts and extreme temperatures.

In general, choosing the correct exposure for bonsai depends on the species, the climate, and the surrounding environment. Therefore, looking closely at the bonsai and changing the display according to its specific needs is essential.

Humidity

Moisture management is critical to bonsai care. An environment that is too dry or humid can cause health problems for the bonsai. There are three main methods of managing humidity: watering, misting, and using a humidifier tray.

To water the bonsai, avoiding watering too much or too little is essential. Generally, it is recommended to water the bonsai when the substrate is dry and to use non-calcareous water.

Misting consists of spraying water on the leaves and trunk of the bonsai to maintain the humidity in the air around the plant. We recommend spraying the bonsai once or twice a day with non-calcareous water.

The humidifier tray uses a tray filled with water on which the bonsai is placed without letting the tree roots touch the water. This method helps maintain humidity around the bonsai.

It is essential to monitor the humidity of the bonsai and adapt humidity management methods according to the plant's specific needs. In addition, the use of non-calcareous water and the regularity of operations are essential to prevent health problems of the bonsai.

Temperature

Temperature is an essential factor in bonsai care. Most bonsai prefer moderate temperatures and cannot tolerate extreme temperatures, whether too hot or too cold.

It can be covered with a protective fabric or sheet to protect the bonsai from frost. Alternatively, you can move the bonsai to a sheltered location, such as a garage or greenhouse, during colder nights.

To protect the bonsai from excessive heat, it can be placed in a shaded area or a cool place, such as an air-conditioned interior or in the shade of a tree. Furthermore, you can reduce watering frequency during the hottest days to prevent the substrate from getting too hot.

In general, it is essential to closely monitor the Temperature around the bonsai and to adapt the plant's location according to its specific needs. Furthermore, protecting the bonsai from extreme temperatures is necessary to ensure the health and beauty of the plant.

Wind and rain can damage the bonsai and compromise its health. Some preventive measures can be taken to protect the bonsai from these weather conditions.

To protect the bonsai from the wind, the plant can be placed in a sheltered area, such as a garden corner or a veranda. In addition, a protective barrier can be created using nets or screens.

To protect the bonsai from the rain, the plant can be placed under a roof or cover, such as an umbrella or a gazebo. The bonsai can be covered with a protective sheet. It is essential to ensure that the fabric does not touch the bonsai directly to avoid damage to the leaves.

It is essential to closely monitor the weather conditions and take the necessary preventive measures to protect the bonsai. Prevention is critical to ensure the health and beauty of the plant.

Chapter 9: The Management of indoor bonsai: artificial lights and Fans for air circulation

In this chapter, we will talk about the management of indoor bonsai, i.e., plants grown inside the house or in closed places such as offices or conference rooms. The cultivation of indoor bonsai requires particular attention, as these plants enjoy different climatic conditions than the external environment. In this chapter, we will explore techniques to ensure the health and beauty of indoor bonsai trees using artificial lights and fans for air circulation.

How to grow bonsai indoors

Indoor bonsai trees need artificial light as they often don't get enough natural light. However, it is possible to use unique lamps to ensure adequate lighting, positioning them at 15-30 cm above the crown of the bonsai and keeping them on for about 12-14 hours a day.

Furthermore, it is essential to maintain a constant temperature in the environment where indoor bonsai is grown. The ideal temperature varies according to the bonsai species. Still, it is generally recommended to maintain a temperature between 18 and 24 degrees Celsius.

To ensure air circulation around the indoor bonsai, fans can be used, which create a constant light current of air. This will help prevent mold and disease growth and ensure a healthy environment for the bonsai.

To cultivate bonsai indoors, it is necessary to guarantee good lighting, a constant temperature, and fans for air circulation. In this way, healthy growth and beauty of the plant can be ensured.

Use of artificial lights for bonsai

Using artificial lights is a widespread option for growing bonsai trees indoors. There are different types of artificial lights available on the market, including fluorescent lamps and LED lights.

Fluorescent lights are less expensive than LED lights but use more energy and generate more heat. LED lights are more costly but last longer, use less energy, and create less heat.

To position the artificial lights, it is essential to place them to cover the entire canopy of the bonsai, keeping them at 15-30cm above the roof. In general, it is recommended to keep the lights on for about 12-14 hours a day to ensure proper lighting.

In summary, artificial lights are a valuable option for indoor bonsai cultivation, and fluorescent lights and LED lights are the two main types of lights available in the market. It is essential to position the lights to cover the bonsai's entire canopy and keep them on for the correct number of hours a day to ensure good lighting.

How to manage air circulation

Air circulation is essential for the health of indoor bonsai, as it prevents the formation of mold and disease. It is possible to manage air circulation using fans and the opening of the windows.

Fans can create a gentle, constant stream of air around the bonsai, helping to prevent mold and disease build-up. In addition, it is possible to place the fans near the bonsai to create a constant but not excessively strong current of air.

Opening windows can improve air circulation naturally. However, it is essential to pay attention to the temperature and humidity of the external environment to prevent the bonsai from being damaged. In general, it is recommended to open the windows only when the external temperature and humidity are like the internal environment where the bonsai is grown.

In summary, you can use fans and open windows to manage the air circulation around your indoor bonsai. However, it is essential to pay attention to the temperature and humidity of the external environment to avoid damage to the plant.

Overheating protection

Overheating can be a problem for indoor bonsai, as they can be exposed to high temperatures from heat sources such as stoves, radiators, and artificial lights. To protect the bonsai from overheating, some preventive measures can be taken.

First, it is essential to closely monitor the temperature around the bonsai and make sure it is within the maximum recommended temperature for that bonsai species. If not, you can move the plant to a more fantastic location or use fans to cool its surroundings.

Furthermore, it is possible to protect the bonsai from excessive solar radiation, which can contribute to overheating. For example, you can place the bonsai away from sun-exposed windows or use curtains or covers to filter out direct solar radiation.

In summary, to protect the bonsai from overheating, it is essential to closely monitor the temperature around the plant and take preventative measures such as moving to a more fantastic location or using fans. Furthermore, it is possible to protect the bonsai from excessive solar radiation by using curtains or covers.

Chapter 10: Preparing for Shows and Exhibits: Showing and Evaluating

In this chapter, we will explore preparing bonsai for exhibitions and displays. Bonsai exhibitions are an excellent opportunity to showcase your art and share the beauty of plants with other enthusiasts. However, preparing for an exhibit takes time, care, and attention to detail. In this chapter, we will explore techniques for presenting bonsai trees effectively and attractively and how to evaluate the quality of bonsai trees on display.

How to prepare bonsai for exhibitions

Preparing bonsai for display requires care and attention to detail to ensure the plant is at its peak beauty and quality. Some essential techniques for designing a bonsai for an exhibition include pruning, wire, and canopy care.

Pruning is critical to the presentation of a bonsai on display. Proper pruning helps define the shape and structure of the plant, making it more attractive and presentable. Therefore, it is essential to prune precisely and carefully, removing the parts of the plant that do not contribute to its beauty.

Using wire is another important technique for preparing a bonsai for an exhibition. The wire is used to shape the plant and make it more harmonious. Therefore, using the wire precisely and delicately is essential to avoid damaging the plant.

Hair care is another essential part of preparing for shows. It is vital to keep the canopy of the bonsai clean and tidy by removing leaves and details of the plant that do not contribute to its beauty. Furthermore, watering and feeding the plant properly is essential to ensure its health and vitality.

To prepare a bonsai for an exhibition, it is essential to carefully prune it, use wire to shape the plant, and take care of the canopy properly. Then, with care and attention to detail, it is possible to present a bonsai on display at its full beauty and quality.

The bonsai exhibition

Exhibiting a bonsai also requires a practical and attractive presentation. The positioning of the plant is essential to ensure that it is visible and well-positioned among the other bonsai on display. Also, it is necessary to choose the proper lighting to bring out the beauty of the plant.

The decoration is another essential part of presenting a bonsai on display. To complete the plant presentation, you can use small decorative elements, such as pebbles, small shrubs, or ceramic accessories. However, it is essential to stay moderate with decoration, as the bonsai should always remain the focal point of the display.

In summary, the presentation of a bonsai on display requires effective positioning and the proper lighting to bring out the beauty of the plant. The decoration can complete the production, but it is essential to do it sparingly to keep attention from the bonsai itself.

How bonsai is rated at exhibitions

The evaluation of the bonsai on display takes place through specific criteria, which vary according to the organization of the exhibition. However, judges generally evaluate bonsai according to four primary standards: nebari, trunk, branches, and crown.

Nebari refers to the base of the plant, where the roots meet the ground. A well-developed nebari indicates good plant stability.

The trunk is evaluated based on its shape, structure, and size. A well-developed box with a harmonious and natural form is considered a strong point for a bonsai on display.

Branches are rated based on location, length, thickness, and shape. In addition, the well-positioned and well-balanced units of the canopy are considered a strength.

The canopy is evaluated based on its shape, density, and symmetry. A well-developed and harmonious crown indicates good care and formation of the bonsai.

In addition, the judges also evaluate the overall health of the plant, its presentation, and the quality of the display.

In summary, evaluating the bonsai on display is based on specific criteria, including nebari, trunk, branches, and crown. Overall, plant health and presentation are also important for evaluation.

Participation in exhibitions

To participate in bonsai exhibitions, knowing the event's regulations is essential. These regulations may vary according to the show's organization but usually concern the bonsai size, the number of plants allowed per participant, and the cultivation techniques permitted.

To participate in a bonsai exhibition, it is usually necessary to register in advance and provide information about the bonsai to be exhibited. Some exhibits also ask for a photo of the plant and information about its history and formation.

Bonsai exhibitions often offer attendees prizes, ranging from token awards to cash prizes. Tips are usually awarded based on the jury's assessment and the judging criteria established by the exhibition.

In summary, knowing the event regulations and registering in advance is essential to participate in bonsai exhibitions. In addition, Bonsai exhibitions often offer prizes to participants, which are awarded based on the evaluation of the judging panel and the judging criteria established by the show.

Chapter 11: The Future of Your Bonsai: maintenance, improvement, and Passion for Bonsai

This chapter deals with the future of your Bonsai, i.e., how to keep the plant healthy and strong over time and continue developing your passion for Bonsai. We will explore some maintenance techniques for caring for your Bonsai and how you can improve it over time. We'll also discuss the importance of keeping your passion for Bonsai alive by exploring the activities and enthusiast communities you can join.

The daily maintenance of the Bonsai

Daily bonsai maintenance is essential to ensure its long-term health and well-being. Three leading practices must be followed regularly to keep your bonsai tree healthy and robust: watering, pruning, and fertilizing.

Watering is essential to provide your Bonsai with the water it needs to survive and grow. Water must be supplied evenly and regularly, considering your plant's specific needs in terms of quantity and frequency. Too dry or too wet soil can be harmful to your Bonsai.

Pruning is a basic bonsai technique that allows you to maintain the shape and size of the plant, eliminating excess or poorly positioned parts. Pruning can be done throughout the year but with care and attention to avoid damaging the plant.

Fertilizing is essential to provide your bonsai tree with the nutrients it needs to grow and thrive. There are different types of fertilizers available, including organic and inorganic fertilizers. Fertilizing must be done carefully and carefully, following the manufacturer's instructions to avoid damaging the plant.

In summary, daily bonsai maintenance requires regular watering, pruning, and fertilizing to ensure the long-term health and well-being of the plant.

Soil moisture control

Soil moisture control is a fundamental aspect of ordinary bonsai maintenance. always Keeping the soil moist but not too wet is essential to ensure plant health.

To check the humidity of the soil, you can use a simple tool called a "bonsai humidity meter" or insert a finger into the ground to a depth of about 2-3 centimeters to evaluate the presence of humidity.

In the case of dry land, it is necessary to water the Bonsai and check that the soil absorbs the water correctly. However, irrigation must be suspended and wait for the earth to dry in case of too wet ground, however, before proceeding with another watering.

It is essential to maintain regular watering, avoiding leaving the plant without water for too long or submerging it with too much water at once. Generally, most Bonsai require regular watering, about once a day during hot weather and every 2-3 days during cold weather.

Furthermore, it is essential to periodically check the state of the roots of the Bonsai, removing any dry or rotten roots and pruning those that are too long. This will encourage the growth of new healthy roots and prevent any disease.

Periodic fertilization

Periodic fertilization is one of the most essential practices for Bonsai's healthy and vigorous growth. Correct fertilization provides the Bonsai with all the nutrients necessary for its growth and maintains the health of the roots.

Here are some more details on periodic fertilization for Bonsai:

Frequency: The frequency of fertilizing depends on the type of fertilizer used. In general, liquid fertilizers are applied once a week, while solid or granular fertilizers are applied every 4-6 weeks.

Dosage: The dosage of the fertilizer depends on the bonsai species and its age. Generally, following the manufacturer's instructions is advisable to avoid giving too much or too little fertilizer.

- **Types of fertilizer:** There are different types of fertilizer for Bonsai, including organic fertilizers and slow-release fertilizers. Choosing the type of fertilizer best suited to the bonsai species and its growth stage is essential.
- **Time of application:** Fertilizing should be done when the Bonsai is in active growth, usually in spring and summer. During autumn and winter, fertilization can be reduced or stopped depending on the bonsai species' needs.
- **Application:** Liquid fertilizers are usually diluted in water and administered through irrigation. Solid or

granular fertilizers are applied to the soil's surface and then watered to make them penetrate the soil.
- **pH Control:** It is essential to monitor the pH of the soil to ensure the Bonsai is getting the necessary nutrients. The ideal pH for most bonsai species is between 6 and 7.

Periodic fertilization is essential for Bonsai's healthy and vigorous growth. However, it is crucial to follow the specific guidelines for the bonsai species and the type of fertilizer used to avoid damage to the roots or the plant itself.

Growth and shape tracking

Monitoring the growth and shape of your Bonsai is an essential aspect of its routine maintenance. Therefore, it is vital to regularly check the trunk, branches, and crown to evaluate the development of the Bonsai and take the necessary actions to keep it healthy.

Regarding growth, it is essential to keep track of how fast the Bonsai grows and intervene when necessary to prevent it from growing too much or too quickly. Furthermore, it is essential to carefully observe the canopy's formation and ensure it is well-distributed and harmonious.

As for shape, it's important to regularly evaluate the trunk and branches to ensure they hold the desired shape and do not bend or break. If problems are noticed, it is essential to take immediate action to avoid irreparable damage to the Bonsai.

Constantly monitoring the growth and shape of your Bonsai allows you to make the right decisions regarding pruning, shaping, and growth management, ensuring the longevity and beauty of your Bonsai over the years.

Regular cleaning of the environment

Regular cleaning of the environment is essential to keeping indoor Bonsai healthy and sound. Dust, pet hair, and other debris can accumulate on the leaves and branches of the Bonsai, hindering photosynthesis and promoting the proliferation of insects and parasites.

To keep the Bonsai clean, dust must be regularly removed from the leaves and parts of the trunk and branches that are accessible. This can be done with a soft cloth or a delicate brush.

Furthermore, keeping the bonsai pots and surrounding soil clean is essential. Removing dead leaves and branches can also help make the bonsai environment more hygienic.

Finally, keeping the area around the Bonsai clean and free of debris is essential. This can help prevent the growth of insects and pests that could attack the Bonsai.

In general, regular cleaning of the Bonsai's environment is a fundamental aspect of its care. It can help keep it healthy and healthy over time.

Removal of the Bonsai, if necessary

Moving your Bonsai can be necessary for various reasons, such as if the plant outgrows its current pot or if its location is no longer ideal. Here are some tips on how to handle a bonsai move:

- **Choosing the new pot:** Choose a pot slightly larger than the current one so the roots have enough room to grow. Make sure the unique pot has drainage holes to avoid waterlogging.
- **Preparation of the new substrate:** The substrate must be prepared carefully, choosing a soil mix suitable for your Bonsai's specific needs. Make sure the substrate is well draining and aerated.
- **Removing the Bonsai from the old pot:** Gently remove the Bonsai from the old pool, avoiding

damaging the roots. Next, remove the old earth from the sources, careful not to hurt them.

- **Root Pruning:** Trim excess roots to maintain a suitable size for the new pot. Remember that cutting the roots too much can damage the Bonsai, so proceed cautiously.
- **Transplanting the Bonsai into the new pot:** Place the Bonsai in the unique pot and fill the space around the roots with the new substrate. Fill all areas well and press the substrate lightly to avoid air bubbles.

Watering and rest: after transplanting, water the Bonsai generously and place it in a cool, shady place for a few days to allow the plant to recover from the transplanting stress.

Remember that moving the Bonsai must be done with care and attention to ensure the survival and health of the plant.

How to improve your Bonsai

Improving your Bonsai takes time, patience, and dedication. However, there are many advanced modeling and cultivation techniques that you can use to grow your Bonsai and improve it.

One of the most advanced bonsai modeling techniques is defoliation, which involves removing leaves to reduce leaf size, stimulate lateral bud growth, and increase branching. Defoliation must be done carefully to avoid damaging the plant.

Another advanced technique is aerial pruning, which allows you to root a top portion of the Bonsai to create a new plant. This technique requires in-depth knowledge of plant structure and can only be performed by experts.

Growing on rocks or a piece of wood can create a natural feel around the Bonsai. However, these techniques require in-depth knowledge of plant cultivation and material selection.

In summary, advanced bonsai modeling and cultivation techniques require knowledge and experience. Defoliation, overhead pruning, and growing on rocks or wood can all be used to enhance your plant and create a natural feel around it.

The passion for Bonsai

A passion for Bonsai can last a lifetime, and to keep this love for the plant alive, there are several activities you can engage in.

Sharing your passion with other bonsai enthusiasts can be a source of inspiration and learning. Many bonsai clubs worldwide provide an opportunity to meet other like-minded people, participate in exhibitions, and share knowledge and ideas.

Learning is a critical element of the passion for Bonsai. Many resources, such as books, videos, and courses, can help you learn new techniques and develop your knowledge of Bonsai.

Discovery is another essential part of the passion for Bonsai. Exploring nature for new bonsai tree species and studying Japanese bonsai culture can be a way to discover new ideas and sources of inspiration.

In summary, a passion for Bonsai can be maintained through sharing your love with other enthusiasts, continuous learning, and discovering new bonsai tree species and ideas.

The passion for Bonsai can be shared with other people who share the same passion. There are many bonsai enthusiasts' clubs, events, and exhibitions where you can meet other bonsai growers. Sharing experiences, knowledge, and techniques can be very helpful in learning and improving one's skills in bonsai cultivation.

Passion for Bonsai requires constant learning. Therefore, it is essential to always stay up to date with new techniques, how to prevent and treat diseases and pests, and how to shape the shape of the Bonsai. Reading books, taking classes, and exchanging ideas with other enthusiasts are all ways to learn more and improve your skills.

A passion for Bonsai can lead to the discovery of new tree species, new modeling techniques, and new ways of appreciating the beauty of nature. Growing a bonsai takes time and patience, but the result is a small tree representing nature in miniature. This discovery of the beauty of nature can lead to greater awareness and attention to nature itself.

The future of your Bonsai

The future of your Bonsai depends on your ability to take care of the plant and make it grow healthy and strong. You can do a few things to ensure your Bonsai has a bright future.

First, it's important to continue caring for your Bonsai through regular watering, pruning, and fertilizing. Then, the plant will grow and develop its characteristic shape over time.

Secondly, you can consider the evolution of your Bonsai through advanced modeling and cultivation techniques, such as defoliation, aerial pruning, and cultivation on rocks or wood.

Finally, to ensure the long life of your Bonsai, it is essential to prevent disease and pests through regular care and safe cultivation techniques.

In summary, the future of your Bonsai depends on your ability to take care of the plant and make it grow healthy and strong. Continue to care for your Bonsai, consider evolution through advanced techniques, and prevent diseases and pests to ensure its long life.

Conclusions

Dear reader,

We have come to the end of "Bonsai for Beginners," and we hope that we have given you a solid foundation of knowledge and techniques for caring for your bonsai. It has been an absolute pleasure guiding you through this fascinating world, and we hope you have learned as much as we have during this experience.

In this book, we have explored the history and philosophy of bonsai, we have learned how to choose the suitable bonsai for your needs, we have explored trunk and canopy cultivation and shaping techniques, we have learned how to prevent and manage diseases and pests, how to manage indoor climate and conditions, and finally, we explored the future of your bonsai.

It is important to remember that bonsai care requires patience and dedication. It takes time to grow your bonsai healthily and harmoniously. Still, seeing your plant flowering and reaching its natural beauty will be worth it.

We encourage you to take care of your bonsai passionately and invite you to explore this fascinating world further. There are many bonsai clubs and online communities where you can meet fellow enthusiasts, share knowledge, and exchange ideas.

Thank you for choosing "Bonsai for Beginners" as your guide on your bonsai growing adventure. We wish you the best and hope we have inspired you to continue learning and growing this excellent plant.

Appendix 1

Bonsai	Origin	Best Climate
Juniper	Asia, Europe, North America	Temperate, Cold
Maple	Asia, North America	Temperate, Cool
Pine	Worldwide	Temperate, Cool
Elm	Asia, Europe, North America	Temperate, Cool
Azalea	Asia, Europe, North America	Temperate, Mild
Serissa	Asia	Subtropical, Mild
Ficus	Asia, Africa	Subtropical, Warm
Bougainvillea	South America	Tropical, Warm
Trident Maple	Asia	Temperate, Cool
Ginkgo	Asia	Temperate, Cool
Olive	Europe, Africa, Asia	Mediterranean, Warm
Chinese Elm	Asia	Temperate, Cool
Wisteria	Asia, North America	Temperate, Mild
Boxwood	Europe, Asia	Temperate, Cool
Crabapple	Asia, North America	Temperate, Cool
Larch	Northern Hemisphere	Temperate, Cold
Black Pine	Japan	Temperate, Cool
Chinese Sweet Plum	Asia	Subtropical, Mild
Bald Cypress	North America	Temperate, Cool
Dawn Redwood	China	Temperate, Cool
Cotoneaster	Europe, Asia	Temperate, Cool
Shimpaku Juniper	Japan	Temperate, Cool
Japanese White Pine	Japan	Temperate, Cool
Japanese Black Pine	Japan	Temperate, Cool
Hinoki Cypress	Japan	Temperate, Cool
Azalea Kurume	Japan	Temperate, Mild
Japanese Maple	Japan	Temperate, Cool
Satsuki Azalea	Japan	Temperate, Mild
Japanese Flowering Apricot	Japan	Temperate, Mild

Appendix 2

Plant species name	Watering	Average age	Average weight
Japanese maple	Moderate	60-70 years	50-80 lbs.
Chinese elm	Moderate	50-60 years	40-70 lbs.
Ficus	Moderate	50-60 years	60-100 lbs.
Juniper	Low	100+ years	100-200 lbs.
Pine	Moderate	50-60 years	100-150 lbs.
Trident maple	Moderate	50-60 years	50-80 lbs.
Bald cypress	High	50-60 years	100-200 lbs.
Redwood	High	100+ years	500-1000 lbs.
Boxwood	Moderate	50-60 years	40-70 lbs.
Serissa	High	20-30 years	5-10 lbs.
Azalea	High	30-40 years	10-20 lbs.
Buttonwood	Moderate	50-60 years	100-150 lbs.
Olive	Moderate	100+ years	200-300 lbs.
Crabapple	Moderate	40-50 years	40-70 lbs.
Elm	Moderate	50-60 years	50-80 lbs.
Cedar	Low	100+ years	200-300 lbs.
Cork oak	Moderate	50-60 years	100-150 lbs.
Black pine	Low	100+ years	100-200 lbs.
Ginkgo	Moderate	50-60 years	80-120 lbs.
Larch	High	50-60 years	80-120 lbs.
Serpentine juniper	Low	100+ years	100-200 lbs.
Red pine	Moderate	50-60 years	80-120 lbs.
Crabapple	Moderate	50-60 years	50-80 lbs.
Spruce	High	50-60 years	80-120 lbs.
Trident maple	Moderate	50-60 years	50-80 lbs.
Hinoki cypress	Moderate	100+ years	200-300 lbs.
Camellia	Moderate	50-60 years	10-20 lbs.
Wisteria	High	20-30 years	20-30 lbs.
Japanese black pine	Low	100+ years	100-200 lbs.

Appendix 3

Bonsai species	Average market price	Average lifespan
Japanese Maple	$50-100	100 years
Juniper	$30-50	50-100 years
Pine	$30-60	100+ years
Chinese Elm	$20-50	50-150 years
Ficus	$20-50	50-100 years
Trident Maple	$30-80	100+ years
Azalea	$50-150	50-100 years
Serissa	$30-50	10-30 years
Boxwood	$20-50	50-100 years
Olive	$50-100	500+ years
Black Pine	$50-100	100+ years
Bald Cypress	$30-50	100+ years
Ginkgo	$50-100	1000+ years
Buttonwood	$50-100	100+ years
Chinese Elm	$20-50	50-150 years
Cherry Blossom	$50-100	50-100 years
Crabapple	$50-150	20-30 years
Trident Maple	$30-80	100+ years
Dwarf Schefflera	$20-50	10-20 years
Boxwood	$20-50	50-100 years
Pyracantha	$30-50	20-30 years
Japanese White Pine	$50-100	100+ years
Cotoneaster	$30-50	20-30 years
Japanese Larch	$30-50	100+ years
Dawn Redwood	$50-100	100+ years
Dwarf Pomegranate	$30-50	5-10 years
Japanese Black Pine	$50-100	100+ years
Yaupon Holly	$20-50	50-100 years
Wisteria	$50-150	50-100 years
Hinoki Cypress	$30-50	100+ years

Support my work

Printed in Great Britain
by Amazon